A FROG'S LIFE

by Irene Kelly

illustrated by Margherita Borin

red-eyed tree frog

 HOLIDAY HOUSE · NEW YORK

What is a frog's life?

Full of leaps and bounds . . .

red-eyed
tree frog

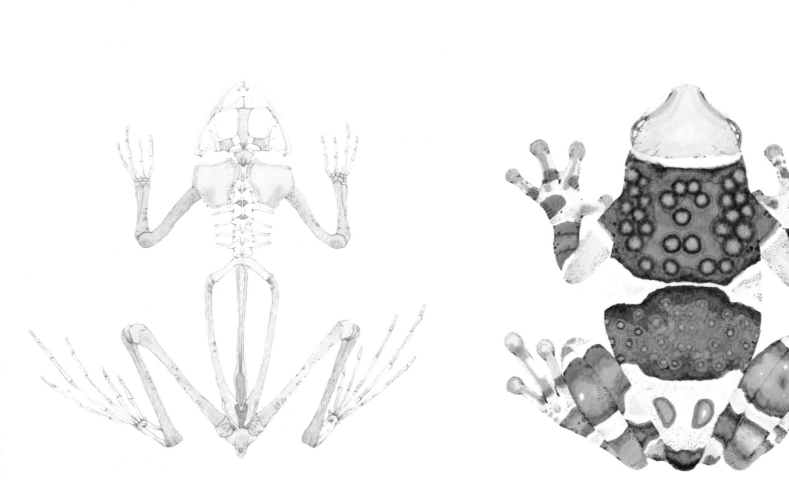

Amazon milk frog

Madagascar tomato frog

Frogs are amphibians—they can live both on land and in water. Frog species have adapted, or changed, over millions of years to be able to survive in their environments. We know there are more than 4,000 types of frogs, but scientists are finding new species all the time.

Amazon milk frog

strawberry poison dart frog

Toads are frogs, too! How can you tell when a frog is a toad? It's easy. Toads spend most of their time on land. They have dry, bumpy skin, short legs, and no teeth. Almost all female toads lay long strands of eggs in water.

Frogs usually live near water, have smooth skin, teeth in their upper jaw, and long, powerful legs, excellent for jumping. The females lay their eggs in clusters in water.

common toad

common
temporaria frog

When frogs are on land, they breathe the same way you do—with their lungs. But when they are underwater, they breathe through their skin.

Oxygen from water can enter a frog's body through its skin, and carbon dioxide can be released through the skin.

Frogs never have to drink. Their skin is like a sponge,
absorbing water as they sit in a pond or swim in a lake.

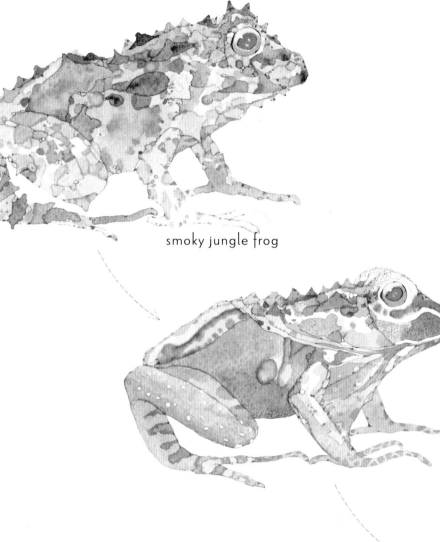

smoky jungle frog

Frogs keep their skin healthy by
shedding it often. Some frogs do this
once a week, others once a day!

The frog stretches, turns, and
"hiccups" to loosen its old skin
and pulls it over its head like
a sweater.

There is a new skin
ready under the old one.

The old skin is full of water and
nutrients . . . so the frog eats it!

ruby-eyed tree frog

wood frog

Some frogs hunt for their food, but many don't—
they simply wait for dinner to come to them.
When a tasty insect flies or crawls by, the frog
shoots out its sticky tongue and nabs it.

But some frogs don't have tongues. Instead, they stuff food into their mouths with their fingers. No frog ever chews—they simply swallow their prey whole.

Some frogs eat just one or two insects every few days, while others consume their entire body weight in bugs daily.

sharp-headed reed frog

Favorite frog foods

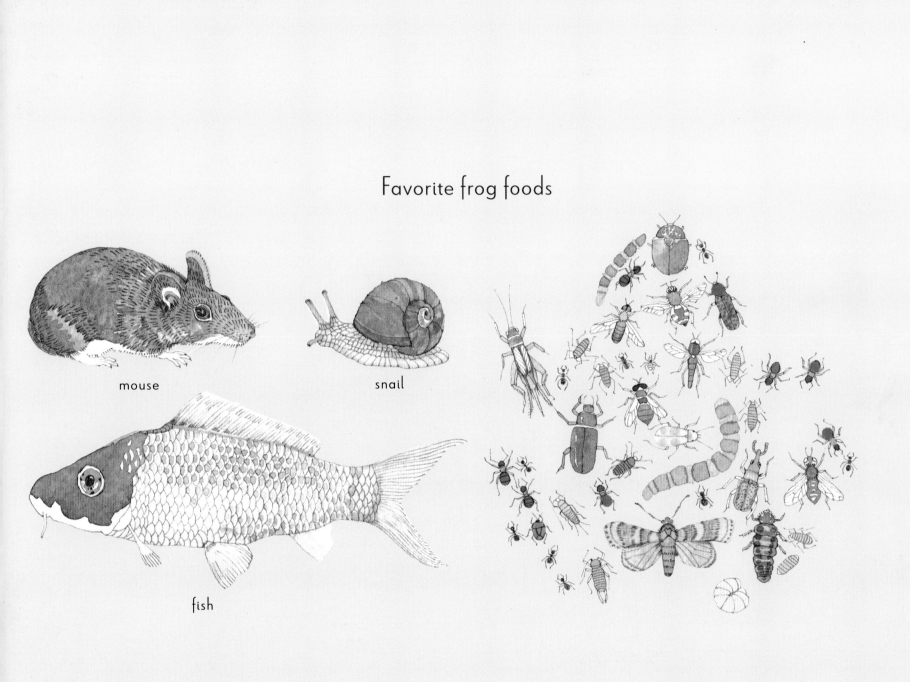

mouse

snail

fish

insects

lizard

turtle

common water frog

snake

Creatures that dine on frogs

Creatures that also eat frogs include
water snakes, large fish, crocodiles,
birds, raccoons, and diving birds.

Frogs have lots of predators.
But they also have strong defenses.

American bullfrog

Frogs have good senses of smell and hearing, helping them to know when a predator is lurking nearby. They don't have necks, so they can't turn their heads. But they can still see what's happening all around them. That's because their bulging eyes sit wide apart on the top of their heads.

Most frogs are expert jumpers, able to escape hungry predators by hopping away. American bullfrogs are especially good at jumping. They can leap more than six feet (nearly 2 meters) in a single bound!

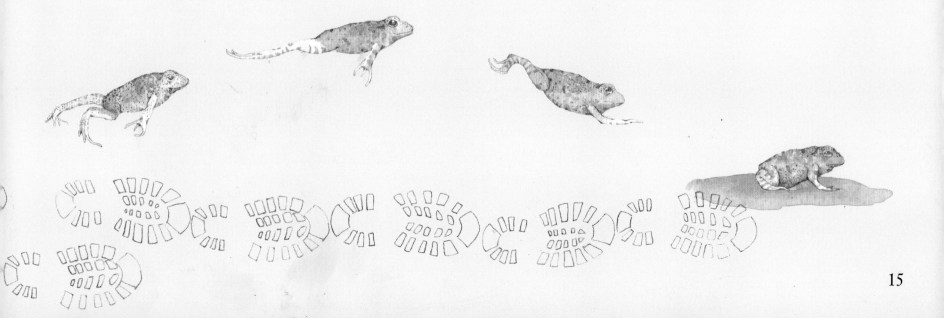

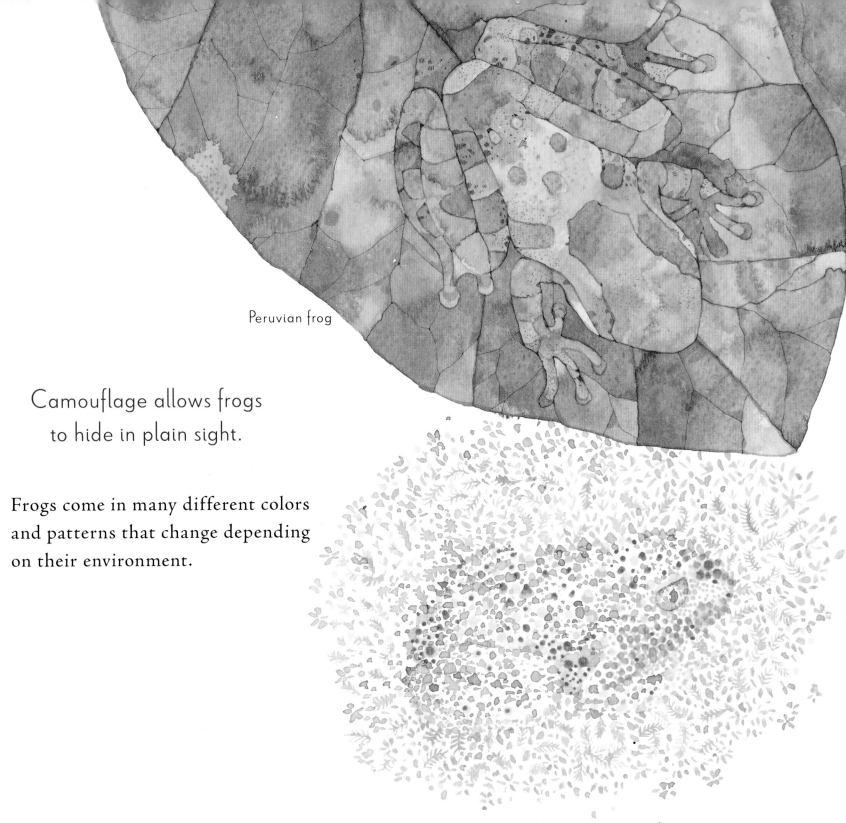

Peruvian frog

Camouflage allows frogs
to hide in plain sight.

Frogs come in many different colors
and patterns that change depending
on their environment.

Vietnamese mossy frog

Many animals won't eat dead animals, so the Darwin frog rolls over and plays dead when it feels threatened.

Darwin frog

The four-eyed frog has two spots near its back legs that look like large eyes. These spots fool predators into thinking the frog is larger than it really is.

four-eyed frog

Each species of frog is perfectly suited to living
in its habitat . . . right down to their toes.

Different types of
frogs have different
types of toes. Frogs
that climb trees
have sticky toes.

red-eyed tree frog

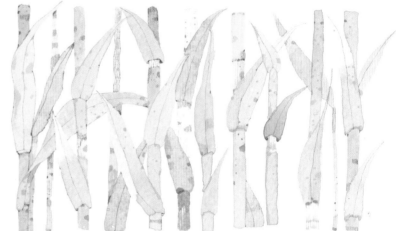

Burrowing frogs
have claw-like toes.

European common frog

Gliding frogs
use webbed
toes like sails.

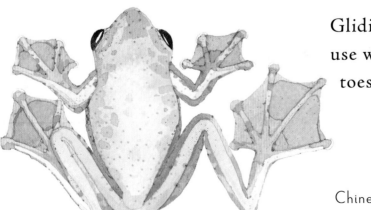

Chinese gliding frog

Chinese gliding frogs
are only 4 inches
(10 centimeters) long,
but they can soar up to
33 feet (5 meters). As this
frog leaps from branch
to branch, it stretches
the webbing between
its toes, turning its
feet into tiny sails.

Chinese gliding frog

Frogs can be found on every continent in the world except Antarctica.
They live in deserts, rain forests, and even on the Arctic tundra.
Some species have had to adapt to survive in harsh climates.

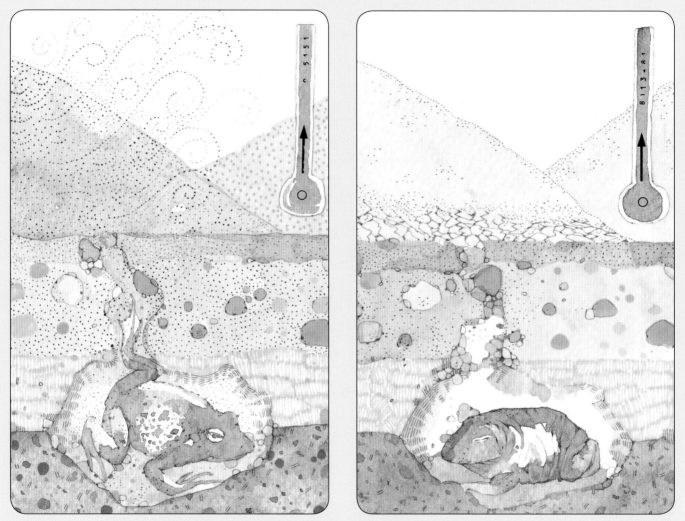

Australian water-holding frog

Australian water-holding frogs live in the desert. When temperatures start to sizzle, they burrow underground, wrapped in cocoons made from their shed skin. They fill their bladders with water and wait for rain—which can take up to seven years to fall!

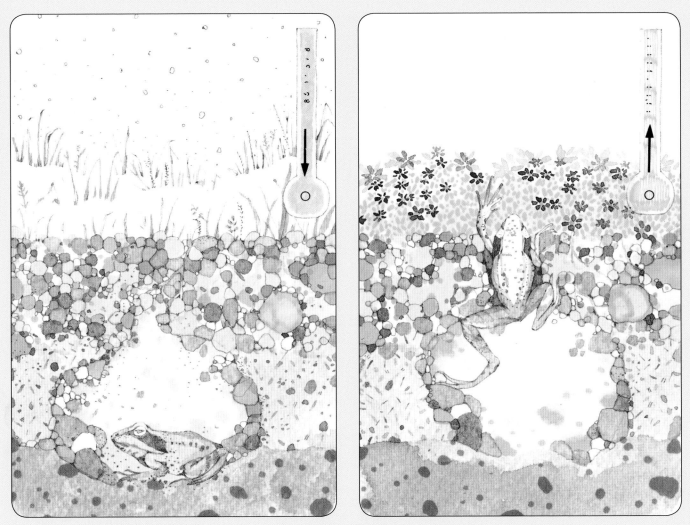

wood frog

The wood frog lives in one of the coldest places on earth, the Arctic. When temperatures drop, this frog goes into a deep freeze. It falls asleep, stops breathing, and its heart stops beating. When spring arrives, the frog thaws out and hops away in search of a mate, as if nothing amazing had happened.

Rain forests are home to more frogs than
any other environment.

American green
tree frog

red-eyed
tree frog

Amazon milk frog

green-bellied
waterfall frog

red frog

Vietnamese
mossy frog

blue dart poison frog

clown
tree frog

giant monkey frog

Madagascar tomato frog

Poisonous frogs store poison in glands just under their skin.

golden poison frog

The Most Poisonous

The bright colors of poisonous frogs warn other animals to stay away. The toxin carried on the skin of a poison dart frog can kill an adult human. The most poisonous animal in the world, the golden poison frog, is only as big as a paper clip, but the toxin it carries can kill 20,000 mice or 10 people.

phyllobates bicolor frog

strawberry poison dart frog

yellow-banded poison dart frog

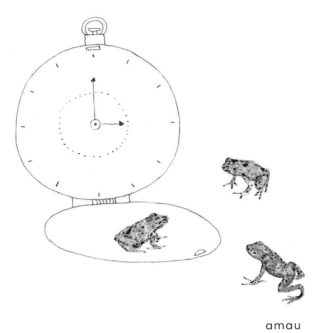

amau

The amau is only as big as a housefly, making it the smallest frog in the world. Its size allows it to live on the ground among leaves, eating tiny insects that are too small for other frogs to bother with.

The largest frog alive today is the goliath toad—and it's a whopper at 2½ feet (75 centimeters) long with its legs stretched out.

goliath toad

Every spring, frogs set off on a journey to find a mate.
They hop along until they reach the pond, lake, or puddle
where they hatched, or they follow the calls of another frog.
Males stake out their territory and launch into their mating songs.

Each species of frog has its own special song. Northern leopard
frogs creak like old doors opening. American toads trill musical
notes. Couch's spadefoot toads bleat like sad sheep. Barking tree
frogs . . . bark! Dancing frogs live under loud waterfalls—their
songs can't be heard. So they dance instead!

barking tree frog

American toad

northern leopard frog

When a female frog hears a male singing, she sings back. The two frogs follow each other's voices until they meet.

The male climbs onto the female's back and hangs on tight to mate with her.

She releases her eggs, and he releases his sperm. The eggs and sperm mix together, fertilizing the eggs. Then the two frogs go their separate ways.

About half of all frog species lay their eggs in clusters in water. There can be up to 35,000 eggs in a single cluster. A jelly coating protects the eggs from bumps and thumps. Baby frogs called tadpoles hatch after 6 to 21 days.

bubble-nest frog

Bubble-nest frogs whip up foamy nests. The female secretes a sticky fluid that the parents whisk with their hind legs, creating a frothy ball. The female lays her eggs in the nest and the male deposits his sperm. The sperm fertilizes the eggs. These nests hang from tree branches over water. As the tadpoles hatch, they drop into the water below.

The female Surinam toad
carries her eggs in pouches
on her back. Skin grows over
them, keeping them safe until
they hatch.

Surinam toad

The strawberry poison dart frog lays eggs
on land. When the tadpoles hatch, they crawl
onto their parent's back and hitch a ride to
water-filled flowers called bromeliads.
They will live in these flowers as
they mature into frogs.

strawberry poison dart frog

raccoon

bird

Tadpoles are popular snacks for
nearly every creature
in their habitat.

baby alligator

snapping turtle

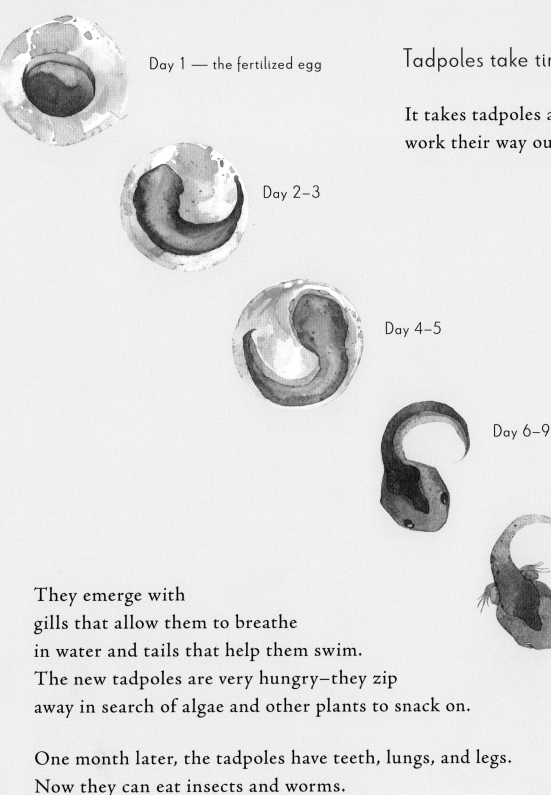

Day 1 — the fertilized egg

Tadpoles take time to develop into adults.

It takes tadpoles a whole day to
work their way out of their eggs.

Day 2–3

Day 4–5

Day 6–9

Day 20–25

They emerge with
gills that allow them to breathe
in water and tails that help them swim.
The new tadpoles are very hungry—they zip
away in search of algae and other plants to snack on.

1 month

One month later, the tadpoles have teeth, lungs, and legs.
Now they can eat insects and worms.

33

1½ months

2 months

After two months, the tadpoles' tails are shorter and their legs are longer.

3 months

At three months old, the tadpoles' tails have disappeared. They breathe air with their new lungs and hop around on their strong legs. They are beginning their lives as frogs.

But they are not done growing. By the time they are adults, they will be 10 times larger than when they first came out of the water.

Frogs have been an important part of our world for a very long time—nearly 250 million years! They help keep our environment healthy by eating large numbers of insects, and they're a food source for other animals.

Mediterranean tree frog

But frogs are in trouble—they are disappearing. This is due to pollution, climate change, and habitat destruction. Their thin skins make frogs very sensitive to pollution. Chemicals like fertilizers invade their watery homes, giving them diseases and often killing them.

It's not hard to find frogs with missing legs or extra legs growing from strange parts of their bodies, such as their stomachs. Is this because of pollution? Scientists don't know for sure but think it's likely.

Climate change is causing the Earth to heat up, and this is bad news for frogs. Because frogs rely on the environment to control their body temperatures, they can't survive big changes in temperature. Warmer climates allow chytrid fungus to thrive on their skins. This disease has already wiped out whole frog species. They are having trouble adapting fast enough to survive this change in their environments.

People are also destroying frog habitats. Every day, 144,000 trees are cut down in rain forests. The wood is used for furniture, flooring, and paper. Land is cleared for cattle to graze. When this happens, frog species lose their homes and become extinct.

Some people think frog legs are delicious. Hundreds of millions of frogs are captured and killed each year for food. Some species have been eaten to extinction.

But there's hope. Scientists all over the world are working hard to save frogs. Many frogs from endangered species have been captured and brought to zoos where they are living and mating. When the frogs' natural habitats are cleaned up, their offspring will be returned to the wild. Conservation programs are saving thousands of frog species.

Index

Page numbers in *italics* refer to illustrations

Here are just a few species that have been rescued:

Archey's frog

blue poison dart frog

Costa Rican variable

dwarf Budgett's frog

golden frog

harlequin toad

leopard frog

Limosa harlequin frogs

orange-bellied frog

Panamanian golden frog

sunset frog

tomato frog

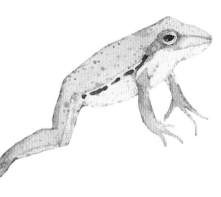

Want to help save frogs? There's plenty you can do.

- Take care of the environment: don't use chemicals in your garden or home. Instead of spraying weeds with poison, pull them out by hand.

- Make sure that wetlands near your home are trash-free.

- Don't keep exotic amphibians as pets.

- And don't eat their legs!

- Join FrogWatch USA and listen for frog songs near your home. By keeping notes on frog songs, you will be helping scientists keep track of frog populations in different parts of the country. http://www.aza.org/become-a-frogwatch-volunteer

- April 28th is Save the Frogs Day! Schools across the globe host a day of fun frog activities and programs to educate the community on the dangers frogs face and how to help them. Talk to your teacher today about how your school can join in.

To Derek and Lucy —I.K.

To Elena —M.B.

The publisher wishes to thank José Rosado of the Harvard University
Museum of Comparative Zoology for his expert review of the text.

Text copyright © 2018 by Irene Kelly
Illustrations copyright © 2018 by Margherita Borin
All Rights Reserved
HOLIDAY HOUSE is registered in the U.S. Patent and Trademark Office.
Printed and bound in December 2017 at Toppan Leefung, DongGuan City, China.
The artwork for this book was made with watercolors, marker pens, and pencils.
www.holidayhouse.com
First Edition
1 3 5 7 9 10 8 6 4 2
Library of Congress Cataloging-in-Publication Data

Names: Kelly, Irene (Irene Kelly Nelson), author. | Borin, Margherita, illustrator.
Title: A frog's life / by Irene Kelly; illustrated by Margherita Borin.
Description: First edition. | New York : Holiday House, 2018.
Identifiers: LCCN 2017006615 | ISBN 9780823426010 (hardcover)
Subjects: LCSH: Frogs—Juvenile literature.
Classification: LCC QL668.E2 K45 2018 | DDC 597.8/9—dc23
LC record available at https://lccn.loc.gov/2017006615

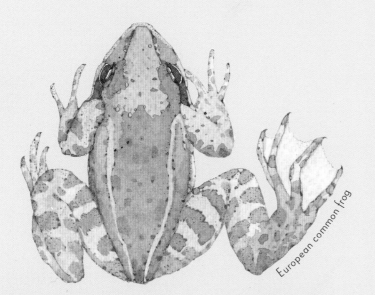

European common frog